Who Is Sleeping?

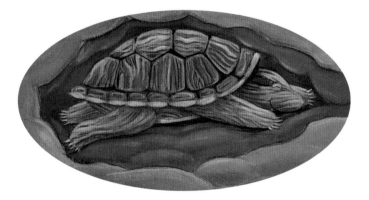

SCHOLASTIC

Children's Press®
A Division of Scholastic Inc.
New York Toronto London Auckland Sydney Mexico City
New Delhi Hong Kong Danbury, Connecticut

Early Childhood Consultants:

Ellen Booth Church
Diane Ohanesian

No part of this publication may be reproduced in whole or in part, or stored in a retrieval system, or transmitted in any form or by any means, electronic, mechanical, photocopying, recording, or otherwise, without written permission of the publisher. For information regarding permission, write to Scholastic Inc., 557 Broadway, New York, NY 10012.

© 2010 Scholastic Inc.

SCHOLASTIC, CHILDREN'S PRESS, ROOKIE PRESCHOOL, and associated logos are trademarks and/or registered trademarks of Scholastic Inc.

1 2 3 4 5 6 7 8 9 10 R 19 18 17 16 15 14 13 12 11 10   62

Library of Congress Cataloging-in-Publication Data

Sapp, Karen.
  Who is sleeping? / Karen Sapp
      p. cm.
  Summary: Illustrations and rhyming text reveal various places in which such animals as chipmunks and bears sleep during the cold and snow of winter.
      ISBN-13: 978-0-531-24411-1 (lib. bdg.)   ISBN-13: 978-0-531-24586-6 (pbk.)
      ISBN-10: 0-531-24411-3 (lib. bdg.)   ISBN-10: 0-531-24586-1 (pbk.)
  1. Stories in rhyme. 2. Animals—Sleep behavior—Fiction. 3. Hibernation—Fiction. 4. Sleep—Fictions. 5. Winter—Fiction. I. Title.

  PZ8.3.S2327Who 2009
  [E] – dc22   2009005500

During winter's ice and snow,

who is sleeping?

Do you know?

When winter turns the woods all white,
some animals sleep out of sight.

4

In a burrow way down deep,
    there is someone fast asleep.
On a brown and leafy bunk,
    sleeps a tiny, striped chipmunk.

In a cave that's dark and deep,
    there are animals fast asleep.
Curled so close their noses rub,
    are a black bear and her cub.

During winter's ice and snow,
who else is sleeping?
Do you know?

Upside down with folded wings,
a sleeping little black bat swings.

During winter's ice and snow,
who else is sleeping?
Do you know?

Under the leaves, beneath the log,

can you find a sleeping frog?

During winter's ice and snow,

who else is sleeping?

Do you know?

Resting there among the leaves,

do you see some fuzzy bees?

During winter's ice and snow,

who else is sleeping?

Do you know?

In a den out of the chill,

sleeps a snake, curled up and still.

During winter's ice and snow,
who else is sleeping?
Do you know?

In the pond in mud below,

someone sleeps far from the snow.

A turtle spends the winter well,

by sleeping tucked inside its shell.

During winter's ice and snow,
who else is sleeping?
Do you know?

Between the rocks—Shhh!—
Don't say a word.
Can you find a sleeping bird?

In the ice and in the snow,
animals know just where to go.

Shhh!

Rookie Storytime Tips

Who Is Sleeping? introduces your preschooler to animals that sleep safe and warm through the cold winter. As you and your child cuddle up to enjoy this book, invite him or her to name the animal on each page before reading the text. It's a great way to reinforce recognition of different types of animals and bolster a key preschool skill.

Invite your preschooler to go back and find the following animals. In exploring the book again, he or she will build knowledge of animal habitats—another piece of the preschool curriculum.

TURTLE

Where does this TURTLE sleep in the winter?

BAT

Where does this BAT sleep in the winter?

BEARS

Where do these BEARS sleep in the winter?

Ask: How do YOU keep warm and cozy when it's cold outside?